She Wished She Could

A Christian Book Series

Shardae' Baye

To order additional copies of this book, contact:
Xlibris
1-888-795-4274
www.Xlibris.com
Orders@Xlibris.com

I first dedicate this book to God. He installed multiple gifts inside of me when he decided that I should be. For that I am forever indebted to him in gratitude. Next, I dedicate this book to my mom, Valerie Davis. She pushed me to use my God given gifts to catapult me to my highest self.

For I know the plans I have for you, declares the LORD, plans to prosper you and not to harm you, plans to give you hope and a future.

Jeremiah 29:11

Shareeta is a little girl who lives in the hood.

She always said "She wish she could."

She dreamed of Thanksgiving and wished for

turkey and ham.

She dreamed of Christmas, she even played in

the Christmas band

By the art museum steps

She played the tuba.

She wished she could.

Shareeta dreamed of her birthday and wished she

was in her very own

backyard swimming pool.

She wished she could be like everyone else and go
to school.

She dreamed of dancing and prancing around

Spain.

She asked Jesus if she could fly in an airplane.

Shareeta often dreamed of food, like potatoes,

collard greens and stew.

Roast fried chicken with stuffing to share.

She even dreamed of wearing pretty cowrie

shells in her hair.

She wished she could, everyday.

She prayed to God that she would be okay.

When Shareeta and her mother lived in a car, she

always wished she

could be a superstar.

Or work on a farm where there was food a plenty.

She wished she could live in a house with a

chimney

She always wished.

Her mother rummaged through the trash
cans for food.
They both ate scraps because they had to.
Shareeta wished she could work at Old
Country Buffet
She wished she could.

Shareeta and her mother went to a shelter

named the Triumphant House.

The Triumphant Holy Church gave them a real bed,
not a hard cot.

Shareeta and her mother got good food a plenty

And her mother began to cry.

No more bridges, no more trash, no more food lines

waiting

No more begging, no more air meals, no more
fasting

No more trash can scraping.

Shareeta and her mother were okay.

God answered her prayers.

No more being homeless

Cause God cares.

Write 6 Reasons Why You Love God

1. _____

_____

2. _____

_____

3. _____

_____

4. _____

_____

5. _____

_____

6. _____

_____

Write 6 Things God Has Done For You

1. _____

_____

2. _____

_____

3. _____

_____

4. _____

_____

5. _____

_____

6. _____

_____

Be on the lookout for these upcoming books from

Mr. and Mrs. Baye!

She Wished She Could Sing, She Wished She

Could Dance, She Wished She

Could Race, She Wished She Could Fly, The

Christian Comic Book Series:

Raheem to the Rescue, Volume 1

ACKNOWLEDGEMENTS

I would like to acknowledge every adult who reads these books. It is very important that we instill a love and desire for Christ in our youth as early as possible. Children need to be reared in Biblical beliefs, informed, as well as instructed on how to put God first in all that they do. It is our duty as believers to lay the foundation of the love and loyalty of Christ our Risen Savior. Let us all be the village to train up the children in the way that they should go. Thank you for supporting my husband and I in advancing the Kingdom.

Printed in the United States
By Bookmasters